Believe

An Odyssey of Faith and Grace

SONYA J. THOMPSON

ISBN 978-1-64416-325-2 (paperback)
ISBN 978-1-64416-327-6 (hardcover)
ISBN 978-1-64416-326-9 (digital)

Christian Faith Publishing, Inc.
832 Park Avenue
Meadville, PA 16335
www.christianfaithpublishing.com

Scripture references are from the New King James Version of the Bible unless otherwise noted.

Printed in the United States of America

Contents

Introduction

It was more than thirty years ago when my odyssey of faith and grace began in West Berlin, Germany. One Sunday morning while showering, preparing to go to the military chapel, I was heavily convicted. Even though I aspired to live a moral life, it hit me; my life was no different than those I criticized and considered hypocrites, just going to church on Sundays. I had never accepted Jesus Christ as my Lord and Savior. I knew of Him, but I didn't know Him. I was at a crossroads and I was compelled to pray. I asked God to make it known to me personally that Jesus Christ was indeed His Son and that He manifest Himself to me. I asked forgiveness for my sins and purposed to read the Bible for myself.

I asked and God answered! He opened my understanding of the scriptures and manifested Himself by transforming my thinking and my way of life. The scriptures became my guide, and I never looked back. I will always remember the first scripture verse God spoke to my spirit: Matthew 6:33, "But seek first the kingdom of God and His righteousness, and all these things shall be added to you." This verse was instrumental in my understanding that when I put God first, following His word, and living His way, then He would take care of all I needed. And He truly has!

Time and time again, I have had to draw strength, comfort, and encouragement from the scriptures to see my way through. And I have continually found that God is true to His word. Whatever the situation or circumstance, God has been faithful to teach, guide, provide, forgive, heal, protect, correct, and to say yes or no according to His will for my good.

I do not always understand the why or the why not nor have things always turned out as I hoped they would, but God has proven faithful to perform what He has promised. The good, the bad, the ugly—He is working it all together for my good and for His glory! And I am assured that He who has begun a good work in me will complete it until the day of Jesus Christ.

The following life experiences I am sharing with you are a testimonial of God's faithfulness and grace to me over the years. As you read the accounts, my prayer is that your faith will be aroused to:

- ❖ Explore and examine the Bible for yourself.
- ❖ Seek intimate fellowship with Jesus Christ.
- ❖ Apply the truth of God's word to your everyday circumstances.
- ❖ Experience the blessing of believing.

> And they overcame by the blood of the Lamb and by the word of their testimony... (Revelation 12:11)

> Jesus said to him, "If you can believe, all things are possible to him who believes." (Mark 9:23)

> God is not a man, that He should lie, nor a son of man, that He should repent. Has He said, and will He not do? Or has He spoken, and will He not make it good? (Numbers 23:19)

> ...Do not be unbelieving but believing. (John 20:27)

Signature of God

A summer evening I set my gaze to observe the German sky
Wanting to contemplate this realm of heavens lights,
But to my dismay only moon rays illumined the night.

Disappointed with a sky bare of starlight fire,
I abandoned my quest and decided to retire.

My thoughts of the barren sky must have been made known,
For on the very next day a heavenly ornament I was shown.

After a common pouring the sun overcame to shine
And along with its brightness the sun revealed a shrine.

Two brilliant arcs adorning the once barren sky
With hues stretching over the mountains high.

A glorious vision my gaze to laud;
The majestic signature of God!

Miraculous Grace

Day Trip

Our family four, off for a day of exploration,
Unaware of the pending divine impartation.
Exercising logic to explain it all away,
But fact and truth testify of what happened on that day.
With little fuel in the tank, no station near in sight,
And many mountainous miles ahead, we ponder at our plight.
Then with cassette player blaring, lifting up His name in praise,
We see the gas gauge rise, and we are all amazed!
Yes, upward from the threatening E, past the
half-full line the indicator went!
We were cruising on a fuel that was heaven sent.
We questioned our eyes but kept right on moving,
Trusting in God's graciousness that He's always proving.
Mile after mile, we drove until we reached our destination,
Never having stopped at a filling station.

This is an account from the mid-1990s when my family was living in Northern Virginia, and my children were still in elementary school—a time before cell phones were prevalent.

Our family was on a day trip to visit Luray Caverns in Virginia's Shenandoah Valley, and in spite of my suggestions that we stop and get gas, we continued on until there were no gas stations in sight. The route we had taken became an isolated mountainous region, and we were very low on fuel. We began to contemplate what we would do when the gas ran out.

All along our journey that day, a cassette tape had been playing by the Brooklyn Tabernacle Choir. So with our eyes on the gas gauge threatening empty, the praises continued to go up when the unexplainable happened. The gas gauge rose to the half-full line and then past the half-full line!

We couldn't believe our eyes! I turned to the back seat and asked the kids to look at the gas gauge and if they could see what had happened and they both replied, "YES!" I just began to thank and praise God and believed He had supernaturally fueled our tank so that we could get to our destination.

We rode for miles until we finally reached the tourist area where there was a gas station. After pulling into the station, before turning the car off, the gas gauge dropped to E.

When I have shared this testimony, some believed and some did not—questioning if the gauge was just malfunctioning. Well, it hadn't malfunctioned prior to the trip, and it never malfunctioned after the trip.

The fact is we didn't start out with enough gas to make the trip from Fort Belvoir, Virginia to Luray, VA which is at least ninety-six miles in distance, approximately a two-hour drive. In the natural order of things, we should have ran out of gas. However, we have a supernatural God who decided to show His loving care and grace with supernatural provision.

I also believe God was protecting us. I hate to think of all the dangers we may have encountered if we had become stranded. Never again did we take a trip without first filling the tank or stopping to get gas when we had the opportunity. Lesson learned—never presume there will be another opportunity!

As I knew then I know now, it was the grace of God that took us to Luray Caverns that day. I don't remember if I prayed for God's help while we were on the road, but I do remember praising Him along with the Brooklyn Tabernacle Choir! And God inhabits the praises of His people (Psalm 22:3, KJV).

God is the source of all resource. He is our provider, and however He chooses to bless us, it will always be in alignment with His word. Throughout the scriptures, there are many examples of God providing supernaturally. One such story is the following account of God's supernatural provision for a widow and His prophet Elijah in a time of drought found in 1 Kings 17:8–16.

Elijah and the Widow

Then the word of the Lord came to him, saying, "Arise, go Zarephath, which belongs to Sidon, and dwell there. See, I have commanded a widow there to provide for you."

So He arose and went to Zarephath. And when he came to the gate of the city, indeed a widow was there gathering sticks. And he called to her and said, "Please bring me a little water in a cup that I may drink." And as she was going to get it, he called to her and said, "Please bring me a morsel of bread in your hand."

So she said, "As the Lord your God lives, I do not have bread, only a handful of flour in a bin, and a little oil in a jar; and see, I am gathering a couple of sticks that I may go in and prepare it for myself and my son, that we may eat it and die."

And Elijah said to her, "Do not fear; go and do as you have said, but make me a small cake from it first, and bring it to me; and afterward make some for yourself and your son. For thus says the Lord God of Israel: 'The bin of flour shall not be used up, nor shall the jar of oil run dry, until the day the Lord sends rain on the earth.'"

So she went away and did according to the word of Elijah; and she and he and her household ate for many days. The bin of flour was not used up, nor did the jar of oil run dry, according to the word of the Lord which he spoke by Elijah.

Read the stories in the Bible of "Elisha and the Widow's Oil" in 2 Kings 4:1–7, of "Jesus turning water into wine" in John 2:1–12, and of "Jesus feeding the five thousand" in Matthew 14:13–21. These accounts, as well as many others, are not recorded just so we will know what He did back then. These accounts were recorded as a witness to the power and unchanging character of God. To strengthen our faith to *believe*.

Take time to meditate on the following scriptures and allow the Holy Spirit to minister to you.

> Whoever offers praise glorifies Me; and to him who orders his conduct aright I will show the salvation of God. (Psalm 50:23)

> But You, O Lord, are a God full of compassion, and gracious, long suffering and abundant in mercy and truth. (Psalm 86:15)

> For your Father knows the things you have need of before you ask Him. (Matthew 6:8)

> And God is able to make all grace abound toward you, that you, always having all sufficiency in all things, may have an abundance for every good work. (2 Corinthians 9:8)

> Grace be with all those who love our Lord Jesus Christ in sincerity. Amen. (Ephesians 6:24)

Healing from Heaven

Fighting the Fever

Baby Steps

Being a young mother and nursing a sick baby is never easy when nothing is working, when you are doing everything you know to do, but your best efforts just aren't enough.

This was the case when my baby boy, Peeper (as I had nicknamed him), had a fever, and his temperature just wouldn't come down. I had followed the doctor's instructions and given him the medicine diligently, but the fever remained. He wasn't sleeping well, and he was irritable. I remember calling the doctor and telling him that the fever was not coming down, and I didn't want to just keep giving my baby all this medicine that wasn't working! He told me to continue giving him the medicine and to give him a cool bath. Well, I did that, and the fever still remained. I was scared for my child, and I needed help that the medicine wasn't providing.

I was not only a young mother at that time, but I was young in the faith as well. And praying for my baby was more of a last resort. So one evening after I had gotten him to sleep, I prayed and asked the Lord to take the fever away and went to bed myself.

Upon waking the next morning, I was alarmed because Peeper hadn't awakened me during the night, which had become normal. I immediately went to the nursery, and to my good pleasure, I found him awake, standing up in his crib, and fever free.

Walking in Faith

As a teenager, my son became ill with a high fever again, but by this time, prayer had become my way of life. One evening as he lie in bed, I laid hands on him and prayed then brought him some cold water to drink. I told him I would come back to check on him and left him to rest.

While showering, I began to pray, and I asked the Lord, just as He rebuked the fever from Peter's mother-in-law and it left her (Luke 4:38–39), to rebuke the fever from my child. I finished showering and got dressed and went back to check on him. And the fever had broken.

The Marathon

I was feeling a little tired but still went on about my normal workday. Then about midafternoon, I started not to feel well and decided to go home. After arriving home, I began to feel worst, and a fever had come on. I took over-the-counter medication and stayed in bed and tried to rest, but my temperature was getting higher. And I began to feel weak. My head was hurting, and my back was aching terribly!

After a few days, I decided I needed to go to the doctor, so I called my son to take me since I was too weak to drive. After seeing the doctor, he suggested that I go to the emergency room, which I did, and I was seen immediately. I was asked a series of questions like if I had been out of the country, and I responded I had not. It was suspected that I may have had meningitis, so I was given the lumbar puncture and admitted to the hospital. The lumbar puncture test came back negative.

My temperature spiked to 104 degrees, and I was given test after test which all came back negative. According to the test, I was in good health! I saw a number of doctors and was given the strongest medication available, but the fever persisted. I didn't want to eat or do anything else.

The fever was so bad that when I closed my eyes I would see the most horrendous creatures and vibrant colors beyond reality. I can't adequately describe the pain and misery I was in.

After being in the hospital approximately four days with the medication not working, I decided to stop the medication and just keep the Intravenous therapy (IV). I had been praying, and my family had asked others to pray with us, but since the medication was not working, I became even more determined in praying because I believed this was a spiritual battle that was manifesting in my physical body. That night, I cried out to the Lord from my hospital bed with all the strength I had, praying for help and relief. Afterwards, I slept.

During the night, a nurse came in my room and asked, "What is going on in here? There is some kind of aura in here."

I thought, *It isn't an aura; it's the Holy Spirit.* Again, I slept.

The next morning, when I awoke, my temperature had come down but rose again as the day progressed, so I continued to pray as others prayed with me. Gradually, my temperature came down and remained normal. After a week in the hospital, I was able to go home, but I was still very weak.

I was out of work for a month regaining my strength, and I know it was only God that brought me through. It was never medically determined what caused my illness.

Pray Mommy, Pray!

You were either seven or eight and the clock read 2:00 when I
was jolted from sleep at your pleading, "Pray, Mommy, Pray"!
I could see your small figure hunched in the dark,
With your arms wrapped around your mid-part.
You began to tell me how awful your stomach hurt
and frantically asking if you would throw up.
I told you to sit and that I would pray but that you should pray too,
Since this was something you needed God to do.
We both said your silent prayers and when I raised
my head you asked, "What did God say?"

And I answered "God didn't say anything, but you will be fine."
That's when you said, "God didn't say it out
loud, but He spoke to my mind."
"He told me I would be okay."
Then you stood straight up and walked away.

I awoke to my son at my bedside bent over in pain, frantic, that he was going to vomit, asking me to pray. After getting up and calming him, we sat at the foot of the bed. I told him I was going to pray and that he should pray too. We prayed silently.

After lifting my head, I saw that my son was watching me, and he asked, "What did God say?" I had to ponder his question before answering because I didn't want to quench his faith, but I had to tell him, "God didn't say anything." Then I continued by saying, "Even though God didn't say anything, didn't mean He wouldn't answer." And I assured him, he would be fine.

What my son stated next truly amazed me! He said, "God didn't say it out loud, but He spoke to my mind, and He told me I would be okay." And he literally stood straight up and walked away. I, on the other hand, had to sit there for a while and process what had just transpired.

God didn't speak to me, but he spoke to my son who first had the faith to believe praying to God would help him and secondly to pray for himself.

God touched his stomach and calmed his fears. Allowing him to go back to bed and sleep through the night; awaking the next morning, ready to go to school!

Jesus said, "Let the little children come to Me, and do not forbid them; for of such is the kingdom of heaven" (Matthew 19:14). Our children need to see us pray so that they will know to do likewise. And it is essential that we encourage our children to pray and seek God for themselves. Out of the mouth of babes and nursing infants He has perfected praise (Matthew 21:16).

There is no situation too minor nor too dire to bring to the Lord in prayer. God is a healer, the Great Physician, and He is able! In the gospel of Mark 10:46–52, we find the following account of Jesus healing blind Bartimaeus.

Jesus Heals Blind Bartimaeus

Now they came to Jericho. As He went out of Jericho with His disciples and a great multitude, blind Bartimaeus, the son of Timaeus, sat by the road begging. And when he heard that it was Jesus of Nazareth, he began to cry out and say, "Jesus, Son of David, have mercy on me!"

Then many warned him to be quiet; but he cried out all the more, "Son of David" have mercy on me!"

So Jesus stood still and commanded him to be called. Then they called the blind man, saying to him "Be of good cheer. Rise, He is calling you."

And throwing aside his garment, he arose and came to Jesus. So Jesus answered and said to him, "What do you want Me to do for you?" The blind man said to Him. "Rabboni, that I may receive my sight." Then Jesus said to him, "Go your way; your faith has made you well." And immediately he received his sight and followed Jesus on the road.

Read the gospel accounts of how Jesus healed the paralytic in Matthew 9:1–8, how He healed a woman with a flow of blood and restored a girl to life in Matthew 9:18–26, and of Jesus healing the two blind men in Matthew 9:27–31. Learn the scriptures and pray the scriptures. God honors His word.

How thankful I am that God still heals through divine intervention as well as through medical professionals and medicine.

Take time to meditate on the following scriptures and allow the Holy Spirit to minister to you.

> For I am the Lord who heals you. (Exodus 15:26)

> O Lord my God, I cried out to You, and You healed me. (Psalm 30:2)

> Blessed is he who considers the poor; the Lord will deliver him in time of trouble. The Lord will strengthen him on his bed of illness; You will sustain him on his sickbed. (Psalm 41:1 & 3)

> Bless the Lord, O my soul, and forget not all His benefits: Who forgives all your iniquities, Who heals all your diseases, Who redeems your life from destruction, Who crowns you with lovingkindness and tender mercies. (Psalm 103:2–4)

> He sent His word and healed them, and delivered them from their destructions. (Psalm 107:20)

> And these signs will follow those who believe . . . They will lay hands on the sick, and they will recover. (Mark 16:17–18)

> And the prayer of faith will save the sick, and the Lord will raise him up. And if he has committed sins, he will be forgiven. Confess your trespasses to one another, and pray for one another, that you may be healed. The effective, fervent prayer of a righteous man avails much. (James 5:15–16)

The Lord Will Provide

Starting Over

After much prayer and consideration, the decision was made. The children and I would remain in the States rather than return to Germany where my husband was stationed. It was December 1997, and I was so thankful to be back in the United States; I was relieved. I had never desired to return to Ohio and live, but now, I was so grateful to be home. I felt safe. I knew the right decision had been made, but I was stepping into the unknown, and I needed the Lord's direction as never before. In Psalms 32:8, the Lord tells us, "I will instruct you and teach you in the way you should go; I will guide you with My eye." And I was depending on Him to do just that.

My primary concern was for my two children, and I didn't want this transition to be disruptive to their education and overall well-being. When I talked to them and explained that we would not be going back to Germany, they actually took it very well. My son expressed a little resistance, but that resistance dissipated quickly. And the decision to remain in the States was accepted. Having my family as a support system helped tremendously.

Since the schools were about to go on winter break, this gave me time to get things figured out before they needed to be enrolled for the New Year. I needed to find us a place to live in a good school district, and I needed to find a new job. In Germany, I was a substitute teacher for the Department of Defense at the American High School, but now, I needed a full time job. We had only packed a suitcase each, so most of our clothes were still in Germany along with our household furnishings and the car.

There was so much to be accomplished. At times, it was overwhelming, but I continually prayed and clung to the promises of God. My mother joined me in prayer each evening, and I was encouraged listening to Christian radio every night while lying in bed. One song that particularly ministered to me was "God Will Make a Way." The lyrics spoke to me as if they had been written for my situation.

My first priority was to find us a place to live. I only had $3,000 in my personal savings account, and I didn't have a job yet. But I remembered I did have a full power of attorney. Before we left Germany, my husband had told me to take it with me. I didn't know why he wanted me to take it, and at the time, I didn't think much about it. However, in hindsight, I know it was God who foreknew what I would need, and He was working on my behalf.

My sister suggested that I look for a place in the suburb where she lived since the school system was highly rated, so I did. I went apartment hunting and found a community near both the middle and high school, and the price was right, so I signed the lease. We would move in approximately a month after we had arrived back in the States.

Since we didn't have any household goods or furnishings, I purchased new bed and bath linens and everything for the kitchen in cash and three rooms of bedroom furniture on credit with no interest if paid off before the promotional period ended, which I did. Now, we just had to wait for the military to ship the living and dining room furniture, our clothes, and other personal belongings. And I would have to go to Bayonne, New Jersey, to pick up my car. My husband and I agreed on the child support that he would send for the children, and there was never a third party involved, a dispute, or a missed payment. God again!

I enrolled the children at the middle school, and it didn't take long for them to adapt to their new educational environment. They made friends and continued to excel academically. However, I knew that all of this was a dramatic change for them since all they had ever known was military life. Now, we were suddenly in the civilian world, and their dad was no longer present. Therefore, I bathed my children in prayer, and I did some fasting as well.

In the midst of getting settled and getting acclimated to our new surroundings, I was also looking for work. At that time, the employment section of the Sunday newspaper was the main source for finding work along with word-of-mouth and having a connection. I was utilizing them all. It was February, and I was still looking for employment. My mother suggested applying to the company she worked for part-time, and I saw their advertisement in the paper. They were hiring with a good starting salary, but the position required working some evenings. And I wanted to be home for the children in the evenings. However, with my mother's encouragement, I decided to apply and just see what happened. No other prospects had materialized, and I needed a job.

After applying, I was called for an interview, then for a second, a third, and finally, a fourth interview with the director. He was very cordial and asked me to tell him about my background. So I began by telling him that I had recently returned to the States with my children from Germany, and he informed me that he was a military brat. We then talked about where we had been stationed, and we both had lived in West Berlin as well as the Military District of Washington, and now, we lived in the same suburb. He told me about the company and the department and stated he was recommending me for the position. Then he went on to say that primetime would be best for me. So I asked him what primetime meant. And he explained that with a primetime schedule, I would still get the same benefits as a full time employee, but I wouldn't have to work a forty-hour week or evenings. Amazing! God had done it again! He was working it all out!

Before I started work on March 21 of 1998, our belongings had arrived from Germany. The household was organized, and I was able to make the trip to New Jersey to pick up my car. The timing was perfect!

I flourished in my position at work, winning numerous awards, and I was promoted several times. And even though I only worked primetime hours, I earned incentive payout almost every month. The children flourished as well, continuing to excel academically while participating in choir, orchestra, track, and basketball. There were still obstacles to overcome, but we were well on our way.

While navigating the course of parenting alone during my children's teenage years, there were some challenges along the way, but the Lord saw us through them all. I realized the only reason that everything had come together the way it had was because of God's faithfulness and grace. He had provided all we needed and more.

Our Source

When you are gainfully employed, it is easy to confuse your employer as your source of provision, when in actuality, they are only a resource from the source, God himself. This is a fact that I had to continually remind myself of after resigning from well-paying positions.

On two occasions, I have left companies because I knew without a doubt, it was time for me to depart, and even though I didn't have another job yet, I resigned. I knew God wouldn't lead me wrong, and I had to trust Him. The plaque in my bathroom that my mother gave me for my birthday one year would serve me well during these times, reminding me, "The will of God will never lead you where the grace of God can't keep you." However, the first time I resigned, it was scary! Even though I had funds in reserve, I needed income before the reserves were depleted. Again, I was stepping into the unknown, believing God had something better for me, and that he would ultimately open the door to where he wanted me. And He did.

During the times when I wasn't working, I didn't want for anything, and all my expenses were paid on time. I never had to borrow a dime. And I attribute this to the financial wisdom I learned from the Bible. I tithed. I had little debt, and I had saved during the time of plenty. The waiting periods between jobs weren't always easy, but I truly learned to wait on the Lord and rest in Him. And employment came through in His time.

In the midst of those waiting periods, it is amazing how the Lord would show me His favor. On one occasion, that favor resulted in a catered Thanksgiving meal for free. The meal had been paid for, but the full price of the meal was refunded to me. My family, my guest, and I enjoyed a delicious Thanksgiving dinner! And all I could say was, "Thank you, Father. I know that was You!"

On another occasion at the end of the year, I prayed and asked the Lord to grant me funds to tithe from before the close of the year as I normally did. Well, no funds had come, and it was December 30, so I thought, *I'll just have to wait until the New Year.* Then that evening, I got a call, and the person told me that the Lord had placed me on their mind. And they wanted to give me a late Christmas gift and an early birthday present in the amount of $2,000.00. I received the funds that evening and was able to give my tithe and offering before the year ended!

God and God alone is our source, and He provides for us through His many resources. The earth is the Lord's, and all its fullness, the world and those who dwell therein (Psalms 24:1). And His provision is all encompassing for the spiritual as well as the material, the tangible and the intangible. He provides wisdom, instruction, our gifts, talents, and abilities, and most importantly, salvation through Jesus Christ. It all comes from Him. Every good gift and every perfect gift is from above, and comes down from the Father of lights, with whom there is no variation or shadow of turning (James 1:17).

However, many times we do not have because we do not ask, and when we do ask, we ask in the wrong way with the wrong motives (James 4:2–3). Ask, and it will be given to you; seek, and you will find; knock, and it will be opened to you. For everyone who asks receives, and he who seeks finds, and to him who knocks it will be opened (Matthew 7:7–8).

And whatever we ask, we receive from Him because we keep His commandments and do those things that are pleasing in His sight. And this is His commandment: That we should believe on the name of His Son Jesus Christ and love one another, as He gave us commandment (1 John 3:22–23).

Now, this is the confidence that we have in Him, that if we ask anything according to His will, He hears us. And if we know that He hears us, whatever we ask, we know that we have the petitions that we have asked of Him (1 John 5:14–15). God is faithful to honor His word!

You Call Me Higher

A continual work You are working in me.
When I think I have learned You call me higher,
Not to trust what I can see or in the systems that seem to be.
To trust You alone for all I need, cautioning me of shameful greed.
As You have been You will continue to be,
My Faithful Provider, My Source, My Testimony.

Take time to meditate on the following Scriptures and allow the Holy Spirit to minister to you.

The—Lord—Will—Provide. (Genesis 22:14)

The Lord is my shepherd; I shall not want. (Psalm 23:1)

Oh, fear the Lord you His saints! There is no want to those who fear Him.
The young lions lack and suffer hunger; but those who seek the Lord shall not lack any good thing. (Psalm 34:9–10)

I have been young, and now I am old; yet I have not seen the righteous forsaken, nor his descendants begging bread. (Psalm 37:25)

For the Lord God is a sun and shield; the Lord will give grace and glory; no good thing will He withhold from those who walk uprightly. (Psalm 84:11)

Be anxious for nothing, but in everything by prayer and supplication, with thanksgiving, let your request be made known to God; and the peace of God, which surpasses all understanding, will guard your hearts and minds through Christ Jesus. (Philippians 4:6–7)

And my God shall supply all your need according to His riches in glory by Christ Jesus. (Philippians 4:19)

For He Himself has said, I will never leave you nor forsake you. (Hebrews 13:5)

Desires of the Heart

College Confirmed

Most every parent wants to see their children get a good education and have a good start in life, and I am no different. My heart's desire was for my children to go to college and to finish, debt free. With both my daughter and son doing well in school, I couldn't bear the thought of them not continuing their education. They were one grade apart in school and would be in college at the same time, and I didn't want either of them to start their adult life in a sinkhole of debt—they'd have to struggle years to get out of.

I knew my savings wouldn't get them through college debt-free, so I determined to pray and to have them pray. All during their high school years when we had family devotions, we'd pray that God would provide the funds for them to go to college and finish debt free.

In my private-prayer time, I would pour out my heart to the Lord for my children; acknowledging it was Him that had given them their intelligence, that it'd not be wasted, and that He allow them to continue their education without going into debt.

I truly believed and still believe the wisdom of the scripture that we should owe no one anything except to love one another (Romans 13:8). Not that I don't believe in credit, I just believe we should avoid being in debt whenever possible.

One Sunday, after having family devotion followed with prayer, my son got up from his knees and said, "I am not going to have to pay for college." He stated it with such certainty. His declaration strengthened my faith, and I was encouraged.

My daughter who is the eldest, by seventeen months, was the first to traverse the college application process. She was accepted into the college that had an excellent program for the field of study she wanted to pursue. However, she wasn't excited to go there, and they didn't offer her any scholarship or financial aid. So I determined to use my savings to get her started and trust God for the rest. I was determined she would not apply for any loans.

Then one day, my daughter came home and said she had spoken with a counselor at school, and he told her, based on her ACT score, she could get a full academic scholarship, and for her to apply and plan a visit to the university. The university also had the program of study she wanted to pursue.

I was skeptical at first, but when the information came in the mail, it was all before me in black-and-white. God had answered our prayers! All four years of her tuition was paid as long as she maintained the required GPA, and I would only have to pay for her room and board. Hallelujah! I had one down and one to go!

My son took honors classes in high school, and he was also a starting basketball player. He wanted to go to school on a basketball scholarship, and he did have schools to express interest in him. However, at my suggestion, he applied to the university his sister attended and was offered a full academic scholarship as well, which he accepted.

In addition to their scholarships from the university, my children were also awarded scholarships through my employer. God had granted me the desire of my heart. And they would be at the same university which would be very beneficial in regards to transportation.

During the first few years at college, my daughter and son shared a 1993 Honda Civic that was ten years old but still reliable to get them around at school and to make the two-hour trek to get home. However, since I was anticipating a move out of state, I knew they would need a new car to travel longer distances. I spoke with their father in regards to helping with a down payment, and he agreed. Now I just had to find a really good deal. So I went to the

Honda dealership that was advertising a sale, offering low monthly payments. I told the salesman, "I wanted to lease a car with the lowest monthly payment possible." And after getting the trade in value for the 1993 Civic along with the down payment, I leased a new 2004 Honda Civic for only $98 a month. The salesman wasn't very happy, but I was ecstatic!

My daughter graduated in May of 2006, and my son graduated in December of 2006, completing his internship and practicum in the spring of 2007. And they both finished completely debt free! Blessed be the name of the Lord!

Looking back, I know God orchestrated it all. If I would have had my way, I would have moved to another suburb of Cleveland while my children where in high school, but nothing was working out in regards to us moving. Every attempt I made to move led to a dead end. I now understand that if we had moved, my daughter would have never had that conversation with the counselor who was instrumental in her getting the scholarship.

"Thank you, Father, for every shut door!"

And we know that all things work together for good to those who love God, to those who are the called according to His purpose (Romans 8:28).

Home, Sweet Home

Driving home from work one evening, observing the familiar surroundings, a singular-penetrating thought impressed my mind. In my spirit, I heard, *It's time to go.*

I had been living in Ohio now for almost seven years. It was now 2004. The children were in college, and I knew it was time for me to move on. I wanted to live in a warmer climate, and I wanted to purchase a new home: A home no one else had lived in, especially, since I had moved so many times as a military spouse. I longed to have my own home, and the request was continually in my prayers.

My thoughts first went to Florida, but after considering, I knew it would be best to choose a place where the company I worked for was located and to just transfer. So I decided I would request a transfer to the Atlanta office.

Before I spoke to anyone at work, I prayed and asked the Lord that His will be done. If it was not for me to go, I prayed that my request would be denied. But if it was His will to give me an open door, I would accept the answer I was given as from Him.

Even though I believed the transfer would be a good move, I wanted to follow the wisdom of Proverbs 3:5–6. Trust in the Lord with all your heart, and lean not on your own understanding; in all your ways acknowledge Him, and he will direct your paths.

So after praying and seeking God first, I decided, rather than speaking to my manager, I would speak to my director about the transfer and what the process would be. I went by his office, and he happened to be available. He invited me to come in, and I explained that I wanted to transfer to the Atlanta office and how I really preferred a warmer climate. He then reminded me that one of my previous directors was now in Atlanta, and that, he would email him and get back to me. He also made it clear that if I did transfer, I would be responsible to pay for the move since it was my request. So I assured him that I was prepared to pay for the move.

Later that same day, my director came to my desk with an email he had printed out. The email was from the director in the Atlanta office and it read, "We'd be happy to have Sonya in Atlanta." He then told me to let him know when I wanted to move. I hadn't gone through any of the normal protocol! This was my open door! I planned a trip to Atlanta, and I only had a weekend to find the right house.

My daughter and sister drove with me to Georgia, and we arrived on a Friday afternoon. A real estate agent had been referred, and the arrangements had been made for us to meet and go house hunting on Saturday. I knew home buying was a process, and I needed to get the ball rolling before returning to Ohio on Monday.

On Saturday, the Realtor and I went from one community to another, and I just wasn't seeing anything that was right for me. With daylight waning, the Realtor drove me back to my hotel, and we agreed to start the search again on Sunday. I was disappointed that I hadn't seen anything I was interested in, and I began to wonder if the trip would be wasted. That night, I prayed, "Lord, I know I didn't come down here for nothing, help me."

Sunday started like how Saturday had ended. Our search wasn't looking very promising, and we were about to head back to the hotel when I saw a sign for a New Pulte Homes community. So we followed the signs to the new community, and when I saw the area, I was encouraged. My daughter was with me this time, and she liked the area as well. We parked in front of the model home, and the Realtor went in first. And they were still open for business.

We toured the model home then the wynward model next door, and I was ready to talk business. The sales representative told me all about the great promotions that were currently being offered. The builder was offering to pay the closing cost along with other promotional options. I was excited. The only thing was how long it would take for the house to be built? The sales representative explained that there was a showcase home, a wynward model, available that a contract had fallen through on, and I should go around the corner and take a look at it.

We drove down the street and around the corner, and found the house with the showcase sign in the front yard, and went in. This was the house I had been looking for! The person who originally contracted to build the house had selected the features I would have chosen for myself. My daughter and I went upstairs, and once I saw the master bathroom, I knew this was my house. I kicked my shoes off and went in the shower. My daughter said, "Mommy, this is it."

We came back down stairs and met the Realtor in the kitchen. I told her that I wanted to purchase the home, and I was pleasantly surprised by her response. She asked that we join hands and pray for God's blessing on the transaction, and that's just what we did.

The sales representative stayed after hours to get all my information, and I signed the purchase agreement. And since the person who first contracted to have the house built had paid the lot premium, my cost for the lot was zero, saving me thousands of dollars!

That was Sunday, July 25, 2004, and I closed on the house Monday, August 30, 2004.

Before leaving the Cleveland office, my director came to my desk and asked me if he could speak with me, and I responded, "Sure." Then followed him back to his office. We both sat, and he stated that I had been a good employee, that he was glad I was staying with the company, and that the company was going to pay for my move. Wow! That was totally unexpected but very much appreciated. And the amount the company allowed for my move surpassed my actual moving cost. I knew this was the hand of God granting me favor. I made my final transition from Ohio to Georgia on Monday, September 20, 2004.

With the blessing of the company paying for my move along with the promotional offers from the builder, I was able to furnish my new house with new furniture, debt free. The only furniture I brought with me from Ohio was the bedroom furnishings. The rest, I was able to give away.

The Little Things

My mother wanted to get her great grandson, my grandson, a train for Christmas, but she hadn't found the type of train she was looking for until I saw a train set online from Macy's. I ordered the train for her and upgraded the shipping, so it would arrive in time for our family Christmas Eve celebration. However, Macy's emailed me to inform me that there was a delay with the carrier, and the train would arrive on Tuesday, December 26. That's when my grandson was leaving to return home!

I called Macy's and got an apology, a refund on the shipping, and a discount but was told there was nothing more they could do. So I reluctantly called my mother to make her aware of the situation, and we both said we were going to pray.

On the Saturday before Christmas Day, December 23, I was in my bedroom when I heard a truck outside then I heard the doorbell ring. So I went downstairs to answer the door. And when I opened the door, there it was, a package from Macy's! My grandson's train set had been sent by UPS Next Day Air Saver!

How awesome is God! Not only did my grandson get his Christmas gift from his Gram-Gram, but my mother and I got a Christmas gift as well!

One of my key verses of scripture is Psalm 37:4–5, which tells us to delight yourself in the Lord and He will give you the desires of your heart. To commit your way to the Lord and trust also in Him and He shall bring it to pass. What does it mean to delight yourself in the Lord? To simply enjoy and take pleasure in our fellowship with Him. Secondly, when we are in fellowship with the Lord, trusting and committing our way to Him, He will give us desires that are in alignment with His will for us. And He will bring it to pass.

In Matthew 15:21–28, read the story of the woman of Canaan whose request to have her demon-possessed daughter healed was initially denied, but how her persistent faith caused Jesus to say, "O woman, great is your faith! Let it be unto you as you desire."

Cause Me to Remember

Thank You Father for inclining to my prayer,
Giving me assurance for my smallest concerns You care.
Keep me always mindful of the grace You have shown.
When I'm battle weary to forgetfulness I'm prone,
But the joy of Your faithfulness makes me battle strong.

Cause me to recall my prayers that seemed to go unanswered,
But for my good You did withhold.
As a shepherd shields a ewe lamb of his fold.
Keep me always mindful of the grace You have shown.
When I'm battle weary to forgetfulness I'm prone,
But the joy of Your faithfulness makes me battle strong.

Take time to meditate on the following scriptures and allow the Holy Spirit to minister to you.

Lord, You have heard the desire of the humble; You will prepare their heart; You will cause Your ear to hear. (Psalm 10:17)

May He grant you according to your heart's desire, and fulfill all our purpose. (Psalm 20:4)

Who is the man who desires life, and loves many days, that he may see good? Keep your tongue from evil, and your lips from speaking deceit. Depart from evil and to do good; seek peace and purse it. The eyes of the Lord are on the righteous and His hears are open to their cry. (Psalm 34:12–15)

Trust in the Lord and do good; dwell in the land and feed on His faithfulness. Delight yourself also in the Lord, and He shall give you the desires of our heart. Commit your way to the Lord, trust also in Him, and He shall bring it to pass. (Psalm 37:3–5)

The fear of the wicked will come upon him, and the desire of the righteous will be granted. (Proverbs 10:24)

If you abide in Me, and My words abide in you, you will ask what you desire, and it will be done for you. (John 15:7)

Now to Him who is able to do exceedingly abundantly above all that we ask or think, according to the power that works in us. (Ephesians 3:20)

Now faith is the substance of things hoped for, the evidence of things not seen. (Hebrews 11:1)

Divine Protection

By My Side

Ministering spirits by my side,
Sent to protect, my celestial guides.
Strengthening me along my journey, aiding me on my way home.
Spiritual battles waged by unseen foes,
Afflicting me with many precarious woes.
I emerge victorious after every encounter,
Thanking the Lord for the help of the heavenly host.
Opposing spirits lurking to lead me astray,
But Abba's warring angels keep me in The Way.
Strengthening me along my journey, aiding me on my way home.

Do not forget to entertain strangers, for by so
doing some have unwittingly entertained angels.
—Hebrews 13:2

It was a Saturday afternoon, and we had taken the hour-and-a-half
drive from Fort Belvoir, Virginia to Harpers Ferry, West Virginia for
an educational family day trip. Upon arrival, we searched the park-
ing lot aisles until we found two open spaces together, so we parked
in the first one, leaving the space open on the passenger side of our
vehicle.

We were just in time to get the bus that was waiting to take
tourist into the lower historic town. And when we boarded, there

was an older couple sitting on the left who greeted us. They were very friendly, and we engaged in polite conversation until the bus left. And then on the way down into the town, the six of us had the bus to ourselves.

After getting off the bus, we began to explore the town, and after a while, we realized that everywhere we went, the couple from the bus followed. Then when my husband was going to take a picture of me and the children, the wife insisted that he get in the picture, and she politely took the camera from him. After retrieving the camera, we walked over to the bridge but then decided not to cross over since it looked like it might rain. And there they were right behind us, deciding not to go across either. It started to feel as if they were our assigned escorts.

They were a very nice couple from what I could tell; however, I began to think, *This is really strange.* So I began to pay close attention to see if they would continue to follow us. And they did. When we decided to catch the bus to go back up to the parking lot area, they decided to leave as well.

After getting off the bus, I told my husband that my daughter and I were going to use the restroom before we got on the road. And yes, we had an escort to the ladies restroom. So when we came out of the restroom and joined my husband and son, I told them, "Something strange is happening here, and do not go anywhere because I wanted to see where this couple was going." Well, the wife joined her husband, and we just stood and watched, and then began to follow them toward the parking lot. They were heading in the direction of our car. They then got into the white car parked on the passenger side of our car! I saw the car back out of the space, but I could not see where the car went.

I was in disbelief! There was no way they could have parked in that space! That space was empty when we parked, and they were already on the bus when we boarded to go down into the town.

Just who that couple was remains a mystery, but I will always remember and ponder our Harpers Ferry escorts.

A Flying Reindeer

While living in Ohio driving home from work one evening, along a very dark suburban road, I would encounter a deer not only in my headlights but in my windshield.

A deer out of nowhere attempting to leap over my vehicle landed on my hood and windshield, bursting through on the passenger side. I screamed at the sight and just held on to the steering wheel while fragments of glass and deer hair pelted the passenger seat. I never stopped driving. The car was never out of control, and somehow, the deer got off of the vehicle. Amazingly, I never felt any impact.

I was shaken, but I continued to drive home. Remarkably, the windshield on the driver's side remained intact. Upon arriving at home, I was not able to open the driver's door, so I had to exit through the passenger side while trying not to get cut. Once I was out of the vehicle, I surveyed the damage, and the driver-side door had been kicked in. The headlight was broken, and the hood was beyond repair. With all the damage, I didn't know how I couldn't have felt some kind of impact, but I hadn't.

Had that deer broken through on the driver's side of the windshield, I would have been completely terrified with glass flying in my face, and more than likely, I would have lost control of the car.

I praised God for His protection that evening and that the impact of the collision was never felt.

The Accident

It happened on my way to work on I-75 South in Marietta. The rush hour traffic was heavy as usual, moving at a moderate pace. Then without notice, the car behind me hit me, and I thought, *okay this is just a fender bender*. When suddenly, I was hit again on the rear end of the driver's side by a tractor trailer truck causing my CRV to spin and turn horizontally on the interstate. All I had time to say was, "JESUS!"

The truck did not stop after hitting me but proceeded down the interstate, ripping the front end of my vehicle apart as it went.

In my mind I was thinking, *HE ISN'T STOPPING!* Then after the truck had passed, I was hit again, and my vehicle spun back to the vertical position and stopped.

The airbag had deployed and burst. Smoke was coming into the vehicle, and I was dazed. A gentleman who had nothing to do with the accident came and tried to open the door to get me out. However, the driver's door had been damaged and couldn't be opened. I called 911, and I called my mother so she could get in touch with my children. The gentlemen told me to try and unlock the passenger door, but I couldn't get it unlocked at first but finally got the lock up. He reached in and pulled me out.

After getting out of the car, I limped a bit when I tried to walk, so the young lady that was in the car behind me had me to sit in her car until the ambulance came. The driver of the truck had stopped further down on I-75 but would not come back to where I was.

A State Trooper arrived on the scene after I was in the ambulance, and he told me he would meet me at the hospital. At the hospital, I began to feel the impact of the accident. My hands were burning! The chemicals from the airbag had gotten on my hands. I didn't realize it, but I had hit my head. And I had multiple bruises on my body.

Both my daughter and son had left work and were in the emergency room with me when the State Trooper arrived. He asked me how I was doing and I responded, "Thankfully, I'm here!" He agreed. He confirmed, what I already knew, that my vehicle was a total loss. He also went over his report and informed me that the truck driver had been cited.

After being fully checked out, I was able to go home, but I would be off work for several days since I hadn't felt the full blow of the accident initially. My body had been thrown out of alignment. Fortunately, I was already scheduled to be on vacation the week following the accident. A cruise had been booked and paid for, and it was questionable if I would be able to go as planned, but thankfully, I was.

It was only because of God's divine protection that my injuries were not worse, and that I didn't lose my life. I believe the heavenly host were dispatched and were there on the interstate with me.

Spiritual Wickedness

Put on the whole armor of God, that you may be able to stand against the wiles of the devil.

For we do not wrestle against flesh and blood, but against principalities, against powers, against the rulers of the darkness of this age, against spiritual host of wickedness in the heavenly places.

Therefore take up the whole armor of God, that you may be able to withstand in the evil day, and having done all, to stand.

Stand therefore, having girded your waist with truth, having put on the breastplate of righteousness,

And having shod your feet with the preparation of the gospel of peace;

Above all, taking the shield of faith with which you will be able to quench all the fiery darts of the wicked one.

And take the helmet of salvation and the sword of the Spirit, which is the word of God;

praying always with all prayer and supplication in the Spirit, being watchful to this end with all perseverance and supplication for all the saints. (Ephesians 6:11–18)

Spiritual warfare is real, and the enemy works supernaturally as well as through people. And I have learned that my best defense against the attacks of the enemy, whatever method he uses, is to be clothed in the full armor of God and to wield the sword of the Spirit which is the Word of God. I also ask the Lord to send His heavenly host.

The most intense spiritual warfare I have ever experienced was when I was confronted with the reality of those involved in the occult. The occult was something I had very little knowledge of, but praise God, He never leaves us ignorant to the devises of the enemy.

I was in a fight with demonic forces. However, because my relationship with the Lord was authentic and I was grounded in the word of God, I was battle ready.

I prayed and asked the Lord, "Why am I going through this when I am your child?"

And He answered, *It is because you are my child.*

Then I was directed to Isaiah 54:4–17, and while reading, the words came off the page resonating in my spirit. I was comforted and encouraged that God was going to see me through. I stayed prayerful, believing God for His help, protection, and deliverance. And I filled the atmosphere with music of praise and victory. At times, I had to declare, "Satan, the blood of Jesus is against you!"

One Sunday, while in the midst of this intense warfare, I went to church for morning service, and a lady, who knew nothing about what I was going through, came to me and said, "You were on my mind all last night, and I have been praying for you."

I almost lost it right there in the chapel, but I contained my emotions. I was so grateful the Lord had someone interceding for me.

None of the wicked devises that were employed against me were effective. And I will never forget when the primary person through whom the enemy was working told me in a most sinister voice, "God really is with you. May He always be with you." Yes, the enemy had to admit that God was with me! What God has blessed, no one can curse!

On at least five other occasions, the Holy Spirit has also made me aware of those involved in occult practices or of contaminated food or drink and for me not to partake. How thankful I am for the leading of the Holy Spirit and God's protection and thankful that no weapon formed against me shall prosper (Isaiah 54:17). It may be formed, but it can never succeed.

> Through the help of the Holy Spirit, I am reminded to look past people, knowing that I don't wrestle with flesh and blood but with spiritual host of wickedness. (Ephesians 6:12)
>
> For though we walk in the flesh, we do not war according to the flesh. For the weap-

ons of our warfare are not carnal but mighty
in God for the pulling down of strongholds.
(2 Corinthians 10:3–4)

I can forgive because God has forgiven
me and I pray for my enemies' salvation. God
did not command me to trust my enemies
but He did command me to love my enemies.
(Matthew 5:44–45)

Therefore, I commit all to Him. Vengeance belongs to the Lord.

Beloved, do not avenge yourselves, but rather
give place to wrath; for it is written, "Vengeance
is Mine, I will repay," says the Lord. Therefore,
"if your enemy is hungry, feed him; if he is
thirsty give him a drink; for in so doing you
will heap coals of fire on his head." Do not be
overcome by evil, but overcome evil with good.
(Romans 12:19–21)

Wherever the enemy has launched his attacks against me, be it a
place of employment, at church, at home, somewhere I was visiting,
or on the road, God has covered me. And whatever devise he has
used against me, be it occult practices, lies, slander, or physical harm,
God has sustained me. And I bless His Holy Name!

But You, O Lord, are a shield for me, my glory and the One
who lifts my head. I cried to the Lord with my voice, and he heard
me from His holy hill. I lay down and slept; I awoke, for the Lord
sustained me (Psalm 3:3–5).

The Lord is my light and my salvation; whom shall I fear? The
Lord is the strength of my life of whom shall I be afraid? When the
wicked came against me to eat up my flesh, my enemies and foes,
they stumbled and fell (Psalm 27:1–2).

The biblical history of Israel, throughout the Old Testament, is
a beautiful narrative of God's divine protection of His people. Read
the story of Balaam and Balak in Numbers chapters 22-24. Balak,

the king of Moab, was determined to have Balaam curse Israel, but he could not. Furthermore, Balaam had to bless Israel at God's command. Another story where God shows His great care of His own is in 2 Kings 6:8–23, when the king of Syria sends a band of raiders for the Prophet Elisha whom God has surrounded with chariots of fire. And one of my very favorites is the story of Queen Esther in the book of *Esther*. It is a must read.

The same protection and help that was available to the people of God in biblical days is available to us today. Read Psalm 91 and Psalm 121, and pray these psalms over yourself.

Take time to mediate on the following scriptures and allow the Holy Spirit to minister to you.

> You prepare a table before me in the presence of my enemies; You anoint my head with oil; my cup runs over. (Psalm 23:5)

> The angel of the Lord encamps all around those who fear Him, and delivers them.

> The eyes of the Lord are on the righteous, and His ears are open to their cry.

> The righteous cry out, and the Lord hears, and delivers them out of all their troubles.

> Many are the afflictions of the righteous, but the Lord delivers him out of them all. (Psalm 34:7, 15, 17 & 19)

> God is our refuge and strength, a very present help in trouble. (Psalm 46:1)

> You, through Your commandments, make me wiser than my enemies…

> You are my hiding place and my shield; I hope in Your word. (Psalm 119:98 & 114)

> The name of the Lord is a strong tower; the righteous run to it and are safe. (Proverbs 18:10)

No weapon formed against you shall prosper, and every tongue which rises against you in judgement you shall condemn. This is the heritage of the servants of the Lord, and their righteousness is from Me, Says the Lord. (Isaiah 54:17)

If God is for us, who can be against us? (Romans 8:31)

Divine Connection

Your Spirit Speaks to Me

On those nights when sleep evades despite how I pursue;
I reluctantly arise and direct my thoughts towards You.
In peace of night when business of day has ceased to be;
These are appointed times Your Spirit speaks to me.
Quietness surrounds me but still Your voice I hear;
Instructing me in Your precepts drawing me in Your presence near.
What wealth would have been forfeited
in the discomfort of my bed,
My soul deprived the joy of having my spirit fed.

I will bless the Lord who has given me counsel;
my heart also instructs me in the night seasons.
—Psalms 16:7

Over the years, there are distinct times when I know that the Holy Spirit was speaking to me. Most of the time, it has been through the reading of His word, listening to a sermon, in prayer, or through song; but there have also been times when He has spoken directly to my mind and spirit.

One particular instance occurred not long after I had dedicated my life to the Lord in West Berlin, Germany. AFN (The Armed Forces Network) was the only American television station, and I would watch the soap operas every afternoon. Until one afternoon, while I was watching, the Holy Spirit posed the question in my mind, *Is this program glorifying to God?* I thought about it, and the program was completely the opposite of what was glorifying to God.

The soap operas were dramas full of deceit, lust, adultery, fornication, and confusion. And none of the characters ever had peace! I began to have such a distaste for the programs; I stopped watching them all together.

The Lord was spiritually maturing me in how NOT to feed my spirit as well as about making wise choices and decisions. That simple question is one in which I would learn to filter everything: IS IT GLORIFYING TO GOD?

I Hear You, I'm Listening

I got the letter you sent.
I heard you over the radio at least three times.
I heard you from the pulpit then through a trusted friend
And you knew just what I needed to hear.
Your piercing voice penetrated my ears.
It's not like I'm hard of hearing; I heard you every time,
But you know me so well, you knew the struggle in my mind.
You always know what's best for me, I assent to that. I do.
Your message came so clearly I am without excuse.
I will not only hear You, but I'll intently listen and attend.

And a Child Shall Lead Them

The Lord has also used my children to assist in growing me up, spiritually speaking. At times, it was very humbling, but the lessons were invaluable. And most of this education took place in their very early years.

When my children were preschoolers, after they would have breakfast, I would read a short Bible story to them. On one particular morning, the story was about the children of Israel complaining in the wilderness after God had brought them out of Egypt. After reading the story, I explained that we are always to be grateful for God's blessing and that we are not to complain.

The day progressed, and while I was cleaning, I began to say how we needed another car, so we wouldn't have to wait on my husband to bring me the car. And that I was tired of all this back-and-forth. Well, my three-year-old daughter walked right over to me, put her hands on her hips, and said, "Mommy! You are just like the children of Israel!"

At first, I couldn't even respond, and when I did, all I could say was, "I hear you, Lord." I had been rebuked by a three-year-old. And I was convicted. The Lord used my daughter to shut my mouth and to be mindful to practice what I was teaching.

There was also an opportunity the Lord used when I was scolding my two-year old son. He had disobeyed my instructions yet again, and I made it clear that I was not pleased. He came to me in tears crying, "Mommy, I'm sorry. I'm sorry!"

And I replied, "No, you are not sorry because you keep on doing it."

And right then, the Lord interrupted my thought and said, *He is sorry. You tell me you're sorry and you sin again.*

Ouch! All I could do was take him in my arms and wipe his tears away.

God has taught me many lessons through motherhood, and one of the richest was in a demonstration of trust.

Trust Me Like That!

He only uttered "Mommy" to put me on notice.
With outstretched arms gleefully leaping,
uninhibited from a midway stair.
My chubby toddler came flying through the air.
The moment I caught him before he could fall,
I realized, it was complete trust that allowed him to fly free.
That's when Abba whispered, *That's how you're to trust Me.*

Throughout the Bible, God communicates with His children by His Spirit. And in the New Testament, the Holy Spirit is the teacher that guides us into all truth. He is the promised Helper from the Father that abides within giving us power to glorify Jesus. The child of God is sealed with the Holy Spirit of promise, who is the guarantee of our redemption (Ephesians 1:13–14).

In the psalms of David and in 2 Samuel 23:2–3, read how the Spirit of the Lord spoke by David and to David. Read about Simeon in Luke 2:25–35 and how the Spirit of the Lord revealed to him that he would not die before he saw Christ and led him to the temple. And of the great outpouring of the Holy Spirit on the Day of Pentecost in Acts chapter 2.

> But you shall receive power when the Holy Spirit
> has come upon you; and you shall be witnesses to
> Me in all Jerusalem, and in all Judea and Samaria,
> and to the end of the earth. (Acts 1:8)

Take time to mediate on the following scriptures and allow the Holy Spirit to minister to you.

> He leads me in the paths of righteousness for His name's sake. (Psalm 23:3)

> Blessed is the man whom You instruct, O Lord, and teach out of Your law. (Psalm 94:12)

> Through Your precepts I get understanding; therefore I hate every false way. Your word is a lamp to my feet and a light to my path.

> The entrance of Your words gives light; it gives understanding to the simple. (Psalm 119:104–105 & 130)

> For whom the Lord loves He corrects, just as a father the son in whom he delights. (Proverbs 3:12)

> However, when He, the Spirit of truth, has come, He will guide you into all truth; for He will not speak on His own authority, but whatever He hears He will speak; and He will tell you things to come.
> He will glorify Me, for He will take of what is Mine and declare it to you. (John 16:13–14)

> Do you not know that you are the temple of God and that the Spirit of God dwells in you? (1 Corinthians 3:16)

> And do not grieve the Holy Spirit of God, by whom you were sealed for the day of redemption. (Ephesians 4:30)

Points to Ponder

The Same Yesterday, Today and Forever

> Jesus Christ is the same yester-
> day, today, and forever.
> —Hebrews 13:8

The God from biblical days is the same God moving and working in our current day and forever. First Corinthians 10:11 tells us, "Now these things happened to them as examples, and they were written for our admonition." So the same God who corrected, directed, healed, delivered, provided, and protected in biblical days will do the same for His children now.

From everlasting to everlasting He is God (Psalm 90:2). And His word has not changed nor will it ever change. As Jesus said, "Heaven and earth will pass away, but My words will by no means pass away" (Matthew 24:35). Therefore, take God at His word. In the power of the Holy Spirit, we can live His word and stand on His promises. God is faithful to do what He has promised. When you seek Him, you will find Him when you search for Him with all your heart (Jeremiah 29:13). The Lord says to call on Him, and He will answer you and show you great and mighty things you do not know (Jeremiah 33:3).

Life More Abundant

> The thief does not come except to
> steal, and to kill, and to destroy. I have
> come that they may have life, and that
> they may have it more abundantly.
> —John 10:10

Jesus told us in John 16:33, "In the world you will have tribulation; but be of good cheer, I have overcome the world." He and He alone can give us a peace surpassing all understanding in this world of turmoil and uncertainty. And though we live in a fallen world corrupted by sin, producing evil, problems, pain, sorrow, and suffering, we can still have abundant life in Jesus Christ.

However, the abundant life does not consist of the lust of the flesh, the lust of the eyes, and the pride of life (I John 2:16–17). And it is so much more than the material things we are so enamored with. For what shall it profit a man if he gains the whole world and loses his own soul? Or what will a man give in exchange for his soul (Matthew 16:26). Our relationship with God should define our lives; not His gifts.

The abundant life is in possessing the fruits of the Spirit: love, joy, peace, long-suffering, kindness, goodness, faithfulness, gentleness, and self-control (Galatians 5:22). For the fruit of the Spirit is in all goodness, righteousness, and truth (Ephesians 5:9). The abundant life is enjoying intimate fellowship with Jesus Christ and walking out your God given purpose in the fruit of the Spirit and having the assurance of a divine birthright beyond this present age.

Blessing of My Fate

In this world where your life is judged by the
abundance of what you possess;
Where wealth and privilege view "others" as somewhat less.
I may be viewed as a commoner, a victim of low estate,
But they don't understand the blessing of my fate.
I don't trust in fleeting riches, nor in earthly
position, to define who I am.
I am of a parentage beyond that of mortal man.
I'm a daughter of His Majesty, with a birthright held in esteem.
Born of the King of kings!
So rejoice beloved siblings akin in the faith;
no matter what your lot may be;
The Providential Hand assures our birthright endures eternity!

The Ultimate Promise

Let not your heart be troubled; you believe in
God, believe also in Me. In my Father's house are
many mansions; if it were no so, I would have
told you. I go to prepare a place for you. And if I
go and prepare a place for you, I will come again
and receive you to Myself; that where I am there
you may be also. (John 14:1–3)

The Lord is not slack concerning His prom-
ise, as some count slackness, but is longsuffering
toward us, not willing that any should perish but
that all should come to repentance. (2 Peter 3:9)

And behold, I am coming quickly, and My
reward is with Me, to give to every one according
to his work. (Revelation 22:12)

This life we now live is temporal and is only a precursor to the life to
come and the eternal destination of our choosing. Without a doubt,

we will all enter into eternity either by death or through the second coming of Jesus Christ. The question is: will we spend eternity with Christ and God the Father or will we be forever separated from Them in outer darkness? The choice is ours to make.

> For God so loved the world that He gave His only begotten Son, that whoever believes in Him should not perish but have everlasting life. For God did not send His Son into the world to condemn the world, but that the world through Him might be saved. (John 3:16–17)

The time we have is invaluable, and we don't know the day of our departure. Nor do we know the day of Christ return, but He did tell us the characteristics of the season and to watch and pray.

> Watch therefore, for you do not know what hour your Lord is coming. Therefore you also be ready, for the Son of Man is coming at an hour you do not expect. (Matthew 24:42 & 44)
>
> For the Lord Himself will descend from Heaven with a shout, with the voice of an archangel, and with the trumpet of God. And the dead in Christ will rise first. Then we who are alive and remain shall be caught up together with them in the clouds to meet the Lord in the air. And thus we shall always be with the Lord. (1 Thessalonians 4:16–17)
>
> He who testifies to these things says, "Surely I am coming quickly." Amen. Even so, come, Lord Jesus! (Revelation 22:20)

Whose Face Will You See?

When you close your eyes in finality whose face will you see?
Will you meet a loved one at the door of eternity?

Will you weep and gnash your teeth, anguished in the residence selected?
Will your soul grieve at arrival because of the gift rejected?

Will you lift your eyes in hell, tormented in the flame?
Will your soul lament in pain with only you to blame?

When you close your eyes in finality whose face will you see?
Will the only Son greet you at your eternal destiny?

Take time to meditate on the following scriptures and allow the Holy Spirit to minister to you.

> The entirety of Your word is truth, and every one of Your righteous judgements endures forever. (Psalm 119:160)

> Jesus said to him, "I am the way, the truth, and the life. No one comes to the Father except through Me." (John 14:6)

> But God demonstrates His own love toward us, in that while we were still sinners, Christ died for us. (Romans 5:8)

> For the wages of sin is death, but the gift of God is eternal life in Christ Jesus our Lord. (Romans 6:23)

> That if you confess with your mouth the Lord Jesus and believe in your heart that God has raised Him from the dead, you will be saved. For with the heart one believes unto righteousness, and with the mouth confession is made unto salvation.

> For "whoever calls on the name of the Lord shall be saved." (Romans 10:9–10 & 13)

> For it is written: "As I live, says the Lord, every knee shall bow to Me, and every tongue shall confess to God. So then each of us shall give account of himself to God. (Romans 14:11–12)

Now I saw a new heaven and a new earth, for the first heaven and the first earth had passed away . . .

"And God will wipe away every tear from their eyes; there shall be no more death, nor sorrow, nor crying. There shall be no more pain, for the former things have passed away." Then He who sat on the throne said, "Behold I make all things new." And He said to me, "Write, for these words are true and faithful." (Revelation 21:1, 4 & 5)

The Odyssey Continues

On the Mountain

I closed my eyes to rest from life and was ushered into another.
High in the mountains I was gazing at a streaming illumination,
In the absence of the sun.
When a voice behind me said,
"That is the throne of God."
Without turning to inquire of whom the voice had come,
I said, "I have to go!" Resolute to move on.
As I went a multitude appeared. Those that were before me,
Further up the path, I'd follow.
Was my faith now sight at last?
Then abruptly I returned, to the life from which I rested,
But my thoughts lingered on the mountain.
And I realized, I had been granted a glimpse of Isaiah's vision.

The word that Isaiah the son of Amoz saw con-
cerning Judah and Jerusalem.

Now it shall come to pass in the latter days
that the mountain of the Lord's house shall be
established on the top of the mountains, and
shall be exalted above the hills; and all the nations
shall flow to it.

Many people shall come and say, "Come and let us go up to the mountain of the Lord, to the house of the God of Jacob; He will teach us His ways, and we shall walk in his paths." For out of Zion shall go forth the law, and the word of the Lord from Jerusalem.

He shall judge between the nations, and rebuke many people; they shall beat their swords into plowshares, and their spears into pruning hooks; nation shall not lift up sword against nation, neither shall they learn war anymore.

—Isaiah 2:1–4

Until that day, my long adventurous journey continues intertwined with history, prophecy, and encounters with those I touch and of those who touch me. The journey has directed my course from living in the shadow of Checkpoint Charlie and the Berlin Wall, which is no more, to the Military District of Washington and the White House and from military spouse to civilian single mother. Each used to advance me on my course of faith and grace.

And still now, the maturation process will not let me be, so as He directs, I willingly proceed. Therefore, each day I press on in anticipation of my next lesson and destination, believing that my latter days will be greater than my former. And I worship Him with my life.

Awaiting

Oh, how I long for that moment foretold,
The promise given centuries ago.
When all God's children meet in the air
And Jesus Himself will beckon us there.
I'm awaiting the sounding that will call me away,
Translating this earthly body of clay.
Taken and changed from this terrestrial form.
Released from all ailment, concern, and grief;
When my soul soars eternally.

About the Author

Believe is Sonya J. Thompson's debut book and was inspired by the family stories that have been recounted over the years of God's faithfulness.

While she has had many professional accomplishments, Sonya considers her two adult children her greatest accomplishment, and she is the proud nana of one grandson, Jeremiah.

She enjoys adding destinations to her travel log and experiencing different cultures, but her greatest enjoyment comes from sharing her faith and making a difference in the lives of those she encounters.

Sonya resides in the Atlanta metro area and considers Georgia home.

You can follow Sonya on her Facebook page Writs of Wisdom.

Writs of Wisdom
By Sonya

facebook.com/Writs-of-Wisdom
writsofwisdom@gmail.com

CPSIA information can be obtained
at www.ICGtesting.com
Printed in the USA
BVHW032139130219
540263BV00001B/29/P

9 781644 163252